William Shakespeare

HAMLET

adapted by

Steven Grant
writer

Tom Mandrake
artist

Gary Fields
letterer

CLASSICS
ILLUSTRATED

 BERKLEY/ FIRST PUBLISHING

The basic story of Hamlet, the vengeance-seeking prince of Denmark, pre-dated William Shakespeare's play by at least 400 years. Shakespeare apparently based his romantic tragedy on a version of the Scandinavian legend that appeared in *Histoires Tragiques* (1576) by Francois de Belleforest, who in turn seems to have relied on Saxo Grammaticus' *Historia Danica* (1200s). Shakespeare may have also drawn from *Ur-Hamlet* (1580s), a play, possibly by the popular playwright Thomas Kyd, that has not survived. It is impossible to determine exactly when Shakespeare completed **Hamlet** and when it was first performed, but written accounts indicate that the first staging took place before 1602. By the time **Hamlet** was staged by Shakespeare's company, the Lord Chamberlain's Men, he had already written more than 20 highly successful plays. Like his other works for the theater, **Hamlet** was written with an eye toward the Globe Theatre's box office; Shakespeare's goal was full houses, not critical success. It is testimony to his genius that Shakespeare achieved both: **Hamlet** was a success from its first opening day, continuing to thrill audiences and readers throughout the years, and is considered by many scholars to be the greatest work of the world's premiere playwright. A poetic, compelling tale of revenge, **Hamlet** also is an insightful examination of the complexity of grief, and of the ageless battle between duty and morality. Several versions of **Hamlet** exist; this adaptation is based on what is generally regarded as the definitive version, a combination of texts that were published in 1604 and 1623.

Hamlet
Classics Illustrated, Number 5

Wade Roberts, Editorial Director
Alex Wald, Art Director

PRINTING HISTORY
1st edition published March 1990

For information, address: The Berkley Publishing Group, 200 Madison Avenue, New York, New York 10016.

ISBN 0-425-12026-0

TRADEMARK NOTICE: Classics Illustrated® is a registered trademark of Frawley Corporation. The Classics Illustrated logo is a trademark of The Berkley Publishing Group and First Publishing, Inc. "Berkley" and the stylized "B" are trademarks of The Berkley Publishing Group. "First Publishing" and the stylized "1F" are trademarks of First Publishing, Inc.

Distributed by Berkley Sales & Marketing, a division of The Berkley Publishing Group, 200 Madison Avenue, New York, New York 10016.

Printed in the United States of America
1 2 3 4 5 6 7 8 9 0

I AM THY FATHER'S SPIRIT, DOOMED FOR A CERTAIN TIME TO WALK THE NIGHT.

AND FOR THE DAY CONFINED TO FAST IN FIRES, TILL THE FOUL CRIMES DONE IN MY DAYS OF NATURE ARE BURNT AND PURGED AWAY.

BUT THIS ETERNAL BLAZON MUST NOT BE TO EARS OF FLESH AND BLOOD. LIST, LIST, O LIST! IF THOU DIDST EVER THY DEAR FATHER LOVE--

REVENGE HIS FOUL AND MOST UNNATURAL MURDER!

MURDER?

MURDER MOST FOUL, AS IN THE BEST IT IS. BUT THIS MOST FOUL, STRANGE AND UNNATURAL.

A SERPENT STUNG ME. SO THE WHOLE EAR OF DENMARK IS BY A FORGED PROCESS OF MY DEATH RANKLY ABUSED.

BUT KNOW, THOU NOBLE YOUTH, THE SERPENT THAT DID STING THY FATHER'S LIFE NOW WEARS HIS CROWN.

O MY PROPHETIC SOUL!

MY UNCLE?!

AY, THAT INCESTUOUS, THAT ADULTEROUS BEAST, WITH WITCHCRAFT OF HIS WIT, WITH TRAITOROUS GIFTS... WON TO HIS SHAMEFUL LUST THE WILL OF MY MOST SEEMING-VIRTUOUS QUEEN.

THUS WAS I, BY A BROTHER'S HAND, OF LIFE, OF CROWN, OF QUEEN AT ONCE DISPATCHED.

O, HORRIBLE! O, HORRIBLE! MOST HORRIBLE!

IF THOU HAST NATURE IN THEE, BEAR IT NOT.

13

15

MY LIEGE, AND MADAM, TO EXPOSTULATE WHAT MAJESTY SHOULD BE, WHAT DUTY IS, WHY DAY IS DAY, NIGHT NIGHT, AND TIME IS TIME, WERE NOTHING BUT TO WASTE NIGHT, DAY, AND TIME.

THEREFORE, SINCE BREVITY IS THE SOUL OF WIT, AND TEDIOUS-NESS THE LIMBS AND OUTWARD FLOURISHES, I SHALL BE BRIEF.

YOUR NOBLE SON IS MAD. MAD CALL I IT--FOR, TO DEFINE TRUE MAD-NESS, WHAT IS'T BUT TO BE NOTHING ELSE BUT MAD? BUT LET THAT GO.

THAT HE IS MAD, 'TIS TRUE: 'TIS TRUE 'TIS PITY, AND PITY 'TIS 'TIS TRUE...

AND NOW REMAINS THAT WE FIND OUT THE CAUSE OF THIS EFFECT --OR RATHER SAY, THE CAUSE OF THIS DEFECT.

PERPEND! I HAVE A DAUGHTER (HAVE WHILE SHE IS MINE), WHO IN HER DUTY AND OBEDIENCE MARK, HATH GIVEN ME THIS.

MORE MATTER, WITH LESS ART.

MADAM, I SWEAR I USE NO ART AT ALL.

"TO THE CELESTIAL, AND MY SOUL'S IDOL, THE MOST BEAUTIFIED OPHELIA--"

THAT'S AN ILL PHRASE, A VILE PHRASE--"BEAUTIFIED" IS A VILE PHRASE.

"IN HER EXCELLENT WHITE BOSOM..."

CAME THIS FROM HAMLET TO HER?

BUT HOW HATH SHE RECEIVED HIS LOVE?

WHAT DO YOU THINK OF ME?

AS OF A MAN FAITHFUL AND HONORABLE.

I WOULD FAIN PROVE SO. BUT WHAT MIGHT YOU THINK, HAD I SEEN THIS HOT LOVE ON THE WING, AND LOOKED UPON IT WITH IDLE SIGHT?

NO, I WENT ROUND TO WORK AND MY YOUNG MISTRESS THUS DID I BESPEAK: "LORD HAMLET IS A PRINCE, OUT OF THY STAR! THIS MUST NOT BE!"

AND HE, REPULSED, A SHORT TALE TO MAKE, FELL INTO A SADNESS... AND INTO THIS MADNESS WHEREIN HE NOW RAVES, AND ALL WE MOURN FOR.

DO YOU THINK 'TIS THIS?

IT MAY BE, VERY LIKE.

HATH THERE BEEN SUCH A TIME --I WOULD FAIN KNOW THAT-- THAT I HAVE POSITIVELY SAID, "'TIS SO," WHEN IT PROVED OTHERWISE?

NOT THAT I KNOW.

BUT LOOK WHERE SADLY THE POOR WRETCH COMES READING.

AWAY, I DO BESEECH YOU, BOTH AWAY!

HOW DOES MY GOOD LORD HAMLET? DO YOU KNOW ME, MY LORD?

EXCELLENT WELL. YOU ARE A FISHMONGER.

NOT I, MY LORD.

THEN I WOULD YOU WERE SO HONEST A MAN.

TO BE HONEST, AS THIS WORLD GOES, IS TO BE ONE MAN PICKED OUT OF TEN THOUSAND.

THAT'S VERY TRUE, MY LORD.

FOR IF THE SUN BREED MAGGOTS IN A DEAD DOG, BEING A GOD KISSING CARRION--

HAVE YOU A DAUGHTER?

I... HAVE, MY LORD.

LET HER NOT WALK I' THE SUN. CONCEPTION IS A BLESSING, BUT NOT AS YOUR DAUGHTER MAY CONCEIVE. FRIEND, LOOK TO 'T!

.., AND GATHER BY HIM, AS HE IS BEHAVED, IF'T BE THE AFFLICTION OF HIS LOVE, OR NO, THAT THUS HE SUFFERS.

OPHELIA, WALK YOU HERE. READ ON THIS BOOK, THAT SHOW OF SUCH AN EXERCISE MAY COLOR YOUR LONELINESS.

WE ARE OFT TO BLAME IN THIS, 'TIS TOO MUCH PROVED, THAT WITH DEVOTION'S VISAGE AND PIOUS ACTION, WE DO SUGAR O'ER THE DEVIL HIMSELF.

ND CAN YOU ... NO DRIFT OF CUMSTANCE ... ST FROM HIM / HE PUTS ON ... CONFUSION, ...TING SO ...RSHLY ALL HIS ... OF QUIET ...H TURBULENT ... DANGEROUS ... LUNACY?

HE DOES CONFESS HE FEELS HIM- SELF DIS- TRACTED, BUT FROM WHAT CAUSE HE WILL BY NO MEANS SPEAK,

WE HAVE CLOSELY ...SENT FOR HAMLET ...ITHER, THAT HE, AS ...WERE BY ACCIDENT, ...MAY HERE AFFRONT OPHELIA.

HER FATHER AND MYSELF WILL SO BESTOW OURSELVES THAT, SEEING UNSEEN, WE MAY OF THEIR ENCOUNTER FRANKLY JUDGE...

O, 'TIS TOO TRUE! HOW SMART A LASH THAT SPEECH DOTH GIVE MY CONSCIENCE. O HEAVY BURDEN!

I HEAR HIM COMING. LET'S WITHDRAW, MY LORD.

THE DEVIL TAKE THY SOUL!

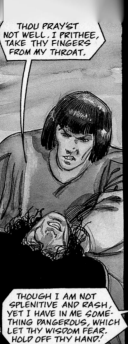

THOU PRAY'ST NOT WELL. I PRITHEE, TAKE THY FINGERS FROM MY THROAT.

THOUGH I AM NOT SPLENITIVE AND RASH, YET I HAVE IN ME SOMETHING DANGEROUS, WHICH LET THY WISDOM FEAR. HOLD OFF THY HAND!

PLUCK THEM ASUNDER

I LOVED OPHELIA! FORTY THOUSAND BROTHERS COULD NOT WITH ALL THEIR QUALITY OF LOVE MAKE UP MY SUM. WHAT WILT THOU DO FOR HER?

HEAR YOU, SIR! WHAT IS THE REASON YOU USED ME THUS? I LOVED YOU EVER. BUT IT IS NO MATTER.

LET HERCULES HIMSELF DO WHAT HE MAY. THE CAT WILL MEW, AND DOG WILL HAVE HIS DAY.

I PRAY THEE, GOOD HORATIO, WAIT UPON HIM.

STRENGTHEN YOUR PATIENCE IN OUR LAST NIGHT'S SPEECH. WE'LL PUT THE MATTER TO THE PRESENT PUSH.

GOOD GERTRUDE, SET SOME WATCH OVER YOUR SON,

THIS GRAVE SHALL HAVE A LIVING MONUMENT. AN HOUR OF QUIET SHALL WE SEE. TILL THEN IN PATIENCE OUR PROCEEDING BE.

SO MUCH FOR THIS, SIR. NOW YOU SHALL SEE THE OTHER. YOU DO REMEMBER ALL THE CIRCUMSTANCE?

UP FROM MY CABIN, MY SEA-GOWN SCARFED ABOUT ME, IN THE DARK GROPED I TO FIND OUT THEM.

HAD MY DESIRE, FINGERED THEIR PACKET, AND IN FINE WITHDREW TO MINE OWN ROOM AGAIN, MAKING SO BOLD TO UNSEAL THEIR GRAND COMMISSION.

WHERE I FOUND AN EXACT COMMAND, LARDED WITH MANY SEVERAL SORTS OF REASONS, IMPORTING DENMARK'S HEALTH, AND ENGLAND'S TOO.

WITH HO! SUCH BUGS AND GOBLINS IN MY LIFE-- THAT, ON THE SUPERVISE, NO LEISURE BATED, NO, NO TO STAY THE GRINDING OF THE AXE, MY HEAD

I SAT ME DOWN, DEVISED A NEW COMMISSION, WROTE IT FAIR.

AN EARNEST CONJURATION FROM THE KING, AS ENGLAND WAS HIS FAITHFUL TRIBUTARY--

--THAT, ON THE VIEW AND KNOWING OF THESE CONTENTS, WITHOUT DEBATEMENT FURTHER, MORE OR LESS--

--HE SHOULD PUT THE BEARERS TO SUDDEN DEATH, NOT SHRIVING TIME ALLOWED.

I HAD MY FATHER'S SIGNET IN MY PURSE, WHICH WAS THE MODEL OF THE DANISH SEAL.

FOLDED THE WRIT UP IN THE FORM OF THE OTHER, SUBSCRIBED IT, GAVE'T THE IMPRESSION, PLACED IT SAFELY, THE CHANGELING NEVER KNOW.

SO GUILDENSTERN AND ROSENCRANTZ GO TO'T.

WHY, MAN, THEY DID MAKE LOVE TO THIS EMPLOYMENT! THEY ARE NOT NEAR MY CONSCIENCE.

WHY, WHAT A KING IS THIS!

DOES IT NOT, THINK'ST THEE, STAND ME NOW UPON? HE THAT HATH KILLED MY KING, AND WHORED MY MOTHER!

AND WITH SUCH COZ'NAGE! IS'T NOT PERFECT CONSCIENCE TO QUIT HIM WITH THIS ARM?

AND IS'T NOT TO BE DAMNED TO LET THIS CANKER OF OUR NATURE COME IN FURTHER EVIL?

IT MUST BE SHORTLY KNOWN TO HIM FROM ENGLAND WHAT IS THE ISSUE OF THE BUSINESS THERE.

IT WILL BE SHORT. THE INTERIM IS MINE. BUT I AM SORRY, GOOD HORATIO, THAT TO LAERTES I FORGOT MYSELF.

BY THE IMAGE OF MY CAUSE I SEE THE PORTRAITURE OF HIS. I'LL COURT HIS FAVORS. BUT SURE THE BRAVERY OF HIS GRIEF DID PUT ME IN A TOW'RING PASSION...

SWEET LORD, IF YOUR LORDSHIP WERE AT LEISURE, I SHOULD IMPART A THING TO YOU FROM HIS MAJESTY.

MY LORD, HIS MAJESTY BADE ME SIGNIFY TO YOU HE HAS LAID A GREAT WAGER ON YOUR HEAD.

SIR, HERE IS NEWLY COME TO COURT LAERTES-- BELIEVE ME, AN ABSOLUTE GENTLEMAN--

WHAT IMPORTS THE NOMINATION OF THIS GENTLEMAN?

YOU ARE NOT IGNORANT OF WHAT EXCELLENCE LAERTES IS -- I MEAN, SIR, FOR HIS WEAPON. IN HIS MEED, HE'S UNFELLOWED.

WHAT'S HIS WEAPON?

RAPIER AND DAGGER--

THAT'S *TWO* OF HIS WEAPONS-- BUT WELL!

LET THE FOILS BE BROUGHT, THE GENTLEMEN WILLING, THE KING HOLDS HIS PURPOSE.

I WILL WIN FOR HIM IF I CAN.

THIS LAPWIG RUNS AWAY WITH THE SHELL ON HIS HEAD.

YOU WILL LOSE THIS WAGER, MY LORD.

I DO NOT THINK SO. SINCE HE WENT INTO FRANCE I HAVE BEEN IN CONTINUAL PRACTICE. I SHALL WIN AT THE ODDS.

IF YOUR MIND DISLIKE ANYTHING, OBEY IT. I WILL FORE-STALL THEIR REPAIR HITHER AND SAY YOU ARE NOT FIT.

NOT A WHIT, WE DEFY AUGURY. SINCE NO MAN HAS AUGHT OF WHAT HE LEAVES, WHAT IS'T TO LEAVE BE-TIMES? LET BE.

COME, HAMLET, COME AND TAKE THIS HAND FROM ME.

GIVE ME YOUR PARDON, SIR. I HAVE DONE YOU WRONG. BUT PARDON'T, AS YOU ARE A GENTLEMAN.

THIS PRESENCE KNOWS, AND YOU MUST NEEDS HAVE HEARD, HOW I AM PUNISHED WITH SORE DISTRACTION.

SIR, IN THIS AUDIENCE, LET MY DISCLAIMING FROM A GENERAL EVIL FREE ME SO FAR IN YOUR MOST GENEROUS THOUGHTS.

I AM SATISFIED IN NATURE, WHOSE MOTIVE IN THIS CASE SHOULD STIR ME MOST TO MY REVENGE.

I DO RECEIVE YOUR OFFERED LOVE LIKE LOVE, AND WILL NOT WRONG IT.

I EMBRACE IT FREELY, AND WILL THIS BROTHER'S WAGER FRANKLY PLAY. GIVE US THE FOILS. COME ON.

COME, ONE FOR ME.

I'LL BE YOUR FOIL, LAERTES. IN MINE IGNORANCE YOUR SKILL SHALL, LIKE A STAR I' THE DARKEST NIGHT, STICK FIERY OFF INDEED.

SET ME THE STOUPS OF WINE UPON THAT TABLE.

IF HAMLET GIVE THE FIRST OR SECOND HIT, OR QUIT IN ANSWER OF THE THIRD EXCHANGE, THE KING SHALL DRINK TO HAMLET'S BETTER HEALTH.

COME, BEGIN. AND YOU, THE JUDGES, BEAR A WARY EYE.

ONE.

NO.

JUDGMENT!

STAY, GIVE ME DRINK. HAMLET, THIS PEARL IS THINE. HERE'S TO THY HEALTH.

GIVE HIM THE CUP.

I'LL PLAY THIS BOUT FIRST. SET IT BY AWHILE.

WILLIAM SHAKESPEARE was baptized in Holy Trinity Church in Stratford-upon-Avon, England, on April 26, 1564. Since the prevailing custom was to christen children three days after birth, Shakespeare is presumed to have been born on April 23, 1564. The third of eight children, Shakespeare was the oldest son born to Mary Arden and John Shakespeare, a prominent shopkeeper who held several local elected offices. Almost nothing is known about Shakespeare's youth and early manhood; it is believed that he attended the local grammar school and then spent several years as a teacher. In 1582, Shakespeare married Anne Hathaway, who was eight years his senior. They had three children: Susanna, born in 1583, and Hamnet and Judith, twins born in 1585. In 1594, Shakespeare joined The Lord Chamberlain's Men London-based troupe as a leading member, and quickly established himself in the city's literary and theatrical community. His relationship with the company (later known as the King's Men) continued throughout his career; the troupe soon developed into London's leading company, occupying both the Globe and the Blackfriars theatres. It is difficult to tell when or in what order Shakespeare wrote his plays. Most scholars agree, though, that Shakespeare began writing for the stage in the late 1580s. His earliest plays apparently include *The Comedy of Errors,* the ambitious *Henry VI* trilogy, *Richard III, Richard II, The Taming of the Shrew,* and *Love's Labour's Lost.* Encouraged, perhaps, by the success of his light-hearted burlesques, Shakespeare then concentrated on a series of comedies, among them *A Midsummer Night's Dream, The Merchant of Venice, Much Ado About Nothing, As You Like It,* and *Twelfth Night.* In his later life, Shakespeare turned again to history and tragedy, composing such plays as *Romeo and Juliet, Henry IV Parts One and Two, Henry V, Julius Caesar, Hamlet, Othello, King Lear, Macbeth,* and *Antony and Cleopatra.* Interspersed among these were his *Sonnets,* and a few comedies and romantic tragi-comedies, such as *All's Well that Ends Well, Measure for Measure,* and *The Tempest.* With an income deriving from three sources — proceeds from the sale of his plays, his wages as an actor, and his share of the company's profits — Shakespeare prospered, enabling him to house his family in Stratford while he spent lengthy periods in London. Around 1611, he resettled in Stratford, retiring in 1613. Shakespeare died on April 23, 1616, and was buried in Holy Trinity Church. His works form the basis for the English theatrical tradition, and remain among the world's favorite plays.

TOM MANDRAKE was born in Ashtabula, Ohio, in 1956. He studied at the Cooper School of Art in Cleveland and the Joe Kubert School of Cartoon and Graphic Art in Dover, New Jersey. His credits include *Batman, New Mutants, Captain Marvel, Swamp Thing, Firestorm,* and *Grimjack.*

STEVEN GRANT was born in Madison, Wisconsin, in 1953. He graduated from the University of Wisconsin, where he studied communication arts and comparative mythology. Grant's comics credits include *Twilight Man, Whisper, Punisher,* and *Life of Pope John Paul II.* The former editor-in-chief of the *Velvet Light Trap Review of Cinema,* Grant has written music criticism for *Trouser Press,* and has contributed to several books on popular culture, including *Close-Ups and The Rock Yearbook.* Grant also has written a variety of widely praised young-adult adventure novels.